Contents

1

emotional intelligence and you

The first step towards achieving good emotional intelligence (EI) is to develop your own emotional self-awareness. This means paying attention to how you are feeling, what you are feeling and why you are feeling it. Instead of simply noticing that you are 'getting emotional', you need to think about exactly what emotions are coming into play – anger, fear, joy, worry, excitement, for example. Knowing exactly what you are feeling will make it much easier for you to develop appropriate reactions to these emotions. Good self-awareness involves being aware of how you are acting and reacting and ensuring that it is in keeping with your values.

Being emotionally intelligent therefore means knowing yourself. It means being able to identify and manage your emotions and to choose and develop your personal values. This opening chapter will focus on helping you to achieve these goals – to develop emotional intelligence by increasing your self-awareness.

Being emotionally intelligent means, first of all, knowing yourself. People with this competence:

* know which emotions they are feeling and why
* realize the links between their feelings and what they think, do and say
* recognize how their feelings affect their performance
* have an awareness of their values and goals.

Being able to accurately assess yourself in these areas is a vital start to making changes. It is important to:

* be aware of your strengths and weaknesses
* be reflective, and be able to learn from past experiences, good and bad
* be open to honest feedback, new perspectives, continuous learning and self-development
* have a good, visible sense of humour and a sense of perspective about yourself.

Identify your own strengths and weaknesses

Here is a test that I give to many of my clients, half of which they find easy, and half of which they find very difficult. I will leave you to guess which is which.

Exercise 1

Take your watch off your wrist and set it beside you. You need to time yourself as you do this test, so don't start until you have made a note of the start time. For the first part of this test, start now.

1 List your top ten weaknesses or faults.

Stop the clock! How long did that take you? Make a note below.

Time taken ☐

Now start the clock again, and complete the second part of this test.

2 List your top ten qualities and strengths.
Stop the clock again. Record your time taken.
Time taken ☐

What have you discovered? I suspect that:

* you found the first part of the test much easier than the second part
* you may have wished for more space for the first part of the test, yet were scratching about to find ten points for the second part
* your time record will show that you took a great deal longer to complete the second part of the test than the first.

What does this tell you?

* That you are a person with hundreds of faults and few good qualities?

Or

* That your view of yourself is pessimistic, and perhaps slanted towards a great deal of self-criticism? In other words, an emotionally unintelligent perception.

The second view is almost certainly going to be your real problem. However, *it actually doesn't matter whether you believe either the first or the second view*. As you will learn, an emotionally intelligent view of yourself doesn't involve considering yourself to be near perfect, but it does involve being both realistic and kind to yourself, rather than pessimistic and harsh.

All that matters is that you are comfortable with yourself – *however you are*. This means that you are looking at yourself in an emotionally intelligent way. Imagine that your negative views of yourself are booming out from a radio. Simply picture the radio in your mind, and then imagine yourself turning the volume down, or fiddling with the tuner button until you find another station.

Recognize the difference between your Ideal Self and your Actual Self

American psychologist Carl Rogers developed a psychological model that he called 'Person-centred'. He believed that everyone has the built-in motivation present to develop their potential to the fullest extent possible. Rogers called this our 'actualizing tendency'. His definition of an emotionally healthy person is that of an emotionally intelligent one (he used his own term, 'fully functioning', but we might well label this as being 'emotionally intelligent'). He stated that each of us has an idea of our Ideal Self – the person we would really like to be. However, most of us have views about ourselves that don't always match our Ideal Selves – and this Rogers called our Real or Actual Self. The more closely our Ideal Self and our Actual Self match, the more healthy (emotionally intelligent) we will be.

The core values that equate to modern emotional intelligence

It is worth looking at Rogers' defined core values for his fully functioning, emotionally intelligent person. Developed by Rogers back in the 1960s, before EI was defined, there are similarities with the work 30 years later of the American psychologist Daniel Goleman. Rogers suggests the following qualities will develop us intelligently:

* **Openness to experience.** This means having an accurate perception of your experiences in the world and being able to accept reality, including your emotions. Rogers emphasizes that being open to your emotions is vital to personal development – his 'self-actualization' is our 'emotional intelligence' (EI).
* **Living in the here and now.** This is the concept of accepting the past and not unduly ruminating over things that have happened and cannot be changed, or placing too much emphasis on an unknown future. It means being

truly present and available within the moment, in order to experience it fully.

* **Trusting ourselves to do what feels right and what comes naturally.** This does not mean going out to commit murder because it 'feels right', but trusting your emotionally intelligent instincts to guide you in the right direction.
* **Using freedom well.** We feel free when choices are available to us. Rogers felt that the fully functioning (emotionally intelligent) person acknowledges such freedom and takes responsibility for their choices.
* **Being creative.** If you feel free and responsible, you will act accordingly, and participate in the world. This can be through creativity in the arts or sciences, through social concern and parental love, or simply by doing your best at your job.

Rogers' emphasis on identifying and being open to emotions is exactly the stuff of modern-day EI. Now test yourself.

Exercise 2

Look at the five qualities listed on pages 6–7 and rate how strongly you believe you possess them yourself.

0 = not at all 5 = quite a lot

Hopefully, you will score reasonably throughout (25 being the highest score; 0 the lowest). If so, this means you have a good baseline EI already, and you are perhaps simply looking to increase it (or you have discovered that you already have EI in abundance and can throw this book away!).

Developing your emotional self-awareness

Emotional self-awareness means giving ongoing attention to your internal state of mind, recognizing what you are feeling and why you are feeling it, and identifying events that can lead to upsets and emotional hijackings. This can mean paying attention to what you see and hear, and not to what you *think* you see and hear.

Emotional hijacking can come about for two reasons:

1. We misinterpret what we hear or what is actually happening. Instead of thinking things through, we jump to a conclusion that then becomes a fact in our minds. We fail to challenge this or check out its accuracy, but simply act on it.
2. We allow ourselves to become so emotionally worked up about what has happened that we lose track of rational behaviour and decision making, and instead fire off on misplaced emotions.

So how do we begin to develop the emotional self-awareness necessary to avoid such confrontations? The answer lies in personal competence. This means knowing yourself and doing the most that you can with what you have. This will give you a consistently wide choice of behaviour options, allowing you to tap in strongly to the parts of your brain that will help you out the most in particular situations.

In order to develop personal competence, you will need to learn:

* to recognize and accurately label your emotions, and to achieve this early enough to be able to control them, before they get out of hand and control you
* to give yourself choices of how to react, rather than letting it be an automatic 'I simply couldn't help it' reaction
* to become more confident in reacting appropriately, so that it becomes second nature to you
* to develop your emotional thinking so that you have a variety of flexible, appropriate ways of responding to situations.

Becoming personally competent is not as difficult as it seems. Remember, you will already have a great number of EI skills and abilities. You are now learning to use these to best effect – to create a better life and opportunities more easily than before.

Start by learning to recognize your emotions

Obviously, what you don't recognize, you can't manage. If you decide that there's nothing wrong, then you won't change. However, to begin with, start thinking about emotions very specifically. We refer to ourselves and/or others as 'getting or becoming emotional'. Now you need to learn to label your emotions very accurately so that you can decide whether or not they are appropriate for a particular situation.

Exercise 3

Write down at least six emotions connected to each of the following:

1 happiness
2 fear
3 anger
4 depression.

A clue to get you started: happiness could involve such emotions as delight, excitement and pleasure.

You need to understand the importance of the above exercise if you are to undertake it with any enthusiasm. What do you think the importance might be? Write your answer down. Now look at the end of the chapter for the answer.

Learning to manage your emotions

Once you are used to identifying and labelling your emotions specifically, you will find it much easier to develop appropriate reactions to them. The example of 'I don't know what came over me' leaves you looking for a solution. However, 'I was overcome with apprehension' gives you valuable information – you might need to deal with what made you apprehensive so that you can handle a similar situation confidently next time.

Self-esteem

William James (1890) defined self-esteem as: 'The feeling of self-worth that derives from the ratio of our actual successes to our pretensions [hopes] for success.' This definition of self-esteem highlights the idea that the way we evaluate ourselves and measure our own sense of self-worth by comparing how we are and how we aspire to be.

What is the difference between self-esteem and self-confidence?

Self-confidence is a result of self-esteem. It is self-esteem in action. If we feel good, we will try more, stretch ourselves more and believe that we can – we are confident enough in our abilities to do so. Self-confident people will:

* present themselves with self-assurance and have 'presence'
* voice views that are unpopular and go out on a limb for what is right
* be decisive and be able to make sound decisions despite uncertainties and pressures.

Self-confidence is the keeper of our actions and reactions. Without it, we can find ourselves acting in a way that we – either at the time or later – may regret. We may find ourselves tongue-tied at a time when we wish to speak eloquently. We may react angrily or defensively when we need to be calm and assertive. We may say too much, say too little, stay when we should go, go when we should stay, and so on. Unless your self-confidence is rock solid and never fails you, you will be familiar with some of these situations.

There are myriad reasons for the onset and development of poor self-confidence. While it is not within the remit of this book to dwell unduly on these, in general many of these reasons can come from childhood criticisms or dysfunctional beliefs that we bring with us into adulthood. Sometimes our confidence is knocked in later life, for example, by the breakdown of a significant relationship, job loss, bereavement or ill health. Any of these things can cause us to lose resilience and feel defeated and unhappy.

The problem is that lack of confidence can be a self-fulfilling prophecy. We don't believe that we can succeed so we don't try. Not trying increases our belief that we are incapable. We can become completely stuck and feel that we have no ability to change our uselessness and lack of ability.

In Chapter 4, we take a look at the enormous power of our thoughts in defining what we do, fail to do, achieve and fail to achieve. You will learn that by changing your thinking, you can change how you feel. You can replace unproductive thinking with emotionally intelligent thinking – and it really will change your life.

Answer to question on page 9: Having a broader choice of emotions to choose from in any given situation will help you to become far more accurate in defining your feelings. Start to discard expressions such as 'I felt awful' or 'I don't know what came over me' and begin to replace them with more accurate definitions like 'I felt filled with remorse' or 'I was overcome with apprehension'. In other words, you will start recognizing your emotions.

2

how to develop emotionally intelligent thinking

What you think decides how you feel. Every time we become emotionally charged about anything, the emotion will be shaped as a result of the thoughts we are having at the time. The more emotionally intelligent we are the more likely it is that our thinking – and thus our emotions – will be accurate and appropriate to the situation. However, our brain often has a mind of its own and fills up with distorted, biased and misguided thoughts that bear little relation to reality and which can lead us to become unnecessarily emotionally upset.

This chapter will teach you how to think more intelligently by learning to evaluate and challenge misguided thoughts and to develop strategies for ensuring that your thinking develops in a more balanced, evaluative and positive way, which in turn will develop more positive and manageable emotions.

EI requires thinking intelligence. Understanding our thinking styles and how we can easily challenge them and change them is an important part of developing EI.

In order to become more intelligent emotionally, therefore, we must also learn to understand the role our thinking styles play in this.

Learning the skills for thought challenging

Thinking types

Our thoughts usually fall into one of four categories:

* positive (where we always see the bright side, true or not)
* evaluative (where we give rational consideration to the options)
* neutral (thoughts that are insignificant, such as what to watch on TV, for example)
* negative (where we see the downside of something and take the bleakest view of a good outcome).

Further, our thoughts, other than the neutral ones, will tend to fall into two further sub-categories:

* self-orientated thoughts (where we spend a great deal of time worrying about outcomes in relation to ourselves)
* action-orientated thoughts (where we decide what we can do about a difficulty that might make a positive difference).

Removing neutral thoughts from the equation, it will be fairly clear that the most productive thoughts to focus on in developing an emotionally intelligent outlook are going to be:

* evaluative thoughts
* action-orientated thoughts.

Understanding that what you think manages your emotions

The way you think has an important effect on the way you feel and what you are able to do. Pessimistic, negative thoughts such as

'I can't cope' or 'I feel terrible' make you feel anxious and unhappy. Some of your thoughts may be based on reality, but some will probably be 'guesswork', and you may be jumping to conclusions that paint things blacker than they are. We call these 'negative automatic thoughts' because they are unrealistically pessimistic and because they seem to come from nowhere and 'automatically' enter your mind. You need to counter this by developing emotionally intelligent thought processes.

Learning to identify negative thoughts

Becoming aware of negative thoughts can help you to understand why you feel the way you do emotionally, and this is the first step towards learning to think in a more helpful, positive way.

To help you become more aware of these thoughts, you first need to know a little more about what negative thoughts 'look like'. The following is a list of characteristics that these thoughts have in common.

* They spring to mind without any effort from you.
* They are easy to believe.
* They are often not true.
* They can be difficult to stop.
* They are unhelpful.
* They keep you anxious and make it difficult to change.

These negative thoughts may be difficult to spot to start with – you are probably not aware that you have them – and the first step is to learn to recognize them.

You can recognize negative thoughts by using a 'Thought record'. The more you practise writing down your thoughts, the easier it becomes to spot them, and to understand the effect they have on your emotions. Don't worry if you find this difficult at first. It may be quite a new idea to try to remember what you were thinking when you were worried or feeling low, and it may take some practice before you get the hang of it. Next time you find yourself becoming emotional in any way, as soon as you can, sit down and write down your accompanying thoughts. Describe the physical sensations you experienced and the thoughts that went through your head at the time.

The way we think changes the way we feel. Never make the mistake of thinking that your emotions pop out of nowhere. Emotions are generated by thoughts – and we always have an opportunity to re-evaluate our thoughts to get a more positive emotional outcome.

What to do when your thoughts aren't clear

Sometimes, it is very difficult for us to access our worrying thoughts, and you may possibly feel that you simply don't know what was in your mind – or you might even feel certain that there was nothing in your mind – it was simply an emotion, sitting there on its own. Don't worry about this, with practice you will gradually learn to access difficult thoughts, and you can also ask yourself some simple questions to assist you. For example, 'What was I afraid might be going to happen?', 'What was happening, or what was in my mind just before I began feeling this way?' or 'Am I recalling any past incidences where things turned out poorly?'

It is not always easy to ascribe emotions to our thoughts. Here are some suggestions to help you:

Am I ...?

anxious	scared	shy	panicky
insecure	sad	hurt	depressed
disappointed	empty	angry	irritated
frustrated	appalled	embarrassed	humiliated
repulsed	sick	nauseous	guilty
ashamed	jealous	envious	shocked
surprised	happy	excited	content
proud			

And there are many more emotions. You can add your own for future reference.

Understanding how your perceptions shape your thoughts

Most people tend to believe that the events in their lives cause them to feel the way they do, i.e. what actually happens is what decides the emotional response. For example, you meet a friend for a drink one evening:

You: Hello, Pete, how are things?

Pete: I feel absolutely dreadful, really bad.

You: Goodness, Pete – whatever has happened to make you feel this way?

Pete: My boss had me in his office this morning to tell me that the report I put together for our biggest client wasn't remotely up to scratch. He was extremely rude and threatened to take me off the account.

Exercise 4

To help you identify emotions specifically, first let's look at Pete's emotional barometer. It's pretty high, but what exactly are his emotions? Feeling 'dreadful', feeling 'bad'. What does this mean?

You can use what you have learned about identifying emotions *specifically* to see that Pete isn't quite giving the helpful information that he could. Take a guess at what emotions might more closely identify with Pete's tale of woe.

This specific identification is really important – you will see why in a moment.

Next, what is it that has made Pete feel this way? Is it:

* the fact that Pete's boss has really laid into him?

Or:

* the meaning that Pete has given to what has happened, i.e. his thoughts about the event and the personal interpretation he has given it?

If Pete's interpretation of the event was that his boss thought he was a useless idiot and Pete agreed with him, then Pete's emotions might be fear ('I'll get the sack or be demoted') or hopelessness ('I'm useless. I'll never get anywhere in life').

If Pete's interpretation of the event was that his boss was being totally unreasonable and exaggerating the poor quality of his work, then Pete's emotions might have been anger ('How dare he speak to me like that?') or frustration ('He never gives me the smallest credit – he always finds a flaw somewhere').

If Pete's interpretation of the event was that his work hadn't actually been quite as good as usual and that his boss was a bit of a tyrant generally, with rarely a good word to say to people, his emotions might have been reasonably calm ('He's right; my work wasn't that good this time so I need to try harder' or 'He shouts at everyone on Monday mornings, it's not personal to me').

In other words, one situation has a variety of possible interpretations and – most importantly – a wide variety of emotional responses.

Learn to challenge negative thoughts

Once you are familiar with identifying negative thoughts and emotions, you can keep track of them and examine how unrealistic or unhelpful they are and whether they are useful to you. If they are unrealistic or unhelpful, you can challenge them with what we call a 'balanced response' (we might also call this an emotionally intelligent response). This is a reply that you can make to these thoughts, based on firm evidence. Studies have shown that doing this can improve your mood and make you feel more in control of your situation and your life.

When you suspect that your thoughts are negative or emotionally upsetting, ask yourself:

* Is this *really* true?
* Is there another way of looking at this?

Write the answers down in your 'Thought record':

Event	*Emotion (rate how strongly you feel it 0–100%)*	*Thought (rate how strongly you believe it 0–100%)*	*Is there another way of looking at this?*
e.g. Getting stood up for a date	Depression (70%) or	'I'm unlovable.' (65%)	'I'm still a great person. They are the idiot.'
	Anger (90%) or	'How dare they?' (80%)	'It's their loss more than mine.'
	Acceptance (100%)	'They probably forgot.' (100%)	'It's possible something has happened to them.'

You should by now have a better idea of how answering your negative thoughts in a more helpful, realistic way can help you to cope with your emotions. However, it can still be hard to think of positive, coping thoughts that will help you deal with your emotions. Here is a list of coping statements that may give you some ideas. Read through the list and think about which of these might apply to you and help you to deal with your emotions in a more positive and constructive way.

Examples of coping statements you might use

* I'm going to face this problem situation so that I can practise coping better.
* It's unlikely that it will work completely, but the important thing is to practise and build up my confidence.
* I know that worry makes me feel worse. I know my feelings can be controlled.
* I've been in this position before and have come out of it alive/still in one piece.

* I know I'll get better the more I get used to coping with worry.
* I'll feel so proud of myself when I feel myself getting calmer.
* It feels good learning how to control worrying feelings.
* I'm deliberately going to change how I feel.

The key to being able to think in a more balanced way is to keep practising. Every time you become aware of negative thoughts going through your mind, try to stop yourself and think of a positive, realistic answer to them.

When preparing to go into a situation that makes you anxious or worried, think about what coping skills you will use (for example, a breathing exercise) and how you will answer any negative thoughts before, during and afterwards. Being prepared is half the battle of helping you to cope.

Making emotionally intelligent thinking your default

One question commonly asked in regard to EI is: Can such a thing really be developed, or are we simply 'born with it' (or not)? There is no doubt that genetic history and parenting style have a huge effect on our abilities to think and respond in certain predefined ways. Yet we are fortunate in the enormous capacity of the human brain to be open to new learning. The key is never to give up.

Imagine you are desperately trying to find a path through the jungle. No matter where you look, you can't see a way through. In the end, you decide to take your machete and simply hack through the undergrowth, which you gradually do. A while later, some others come through the same area of the jungle, also looking for a way through. Eventually, they see the thin trail you have hacked, and they tread the same path, cutting down more branches as they go.

Soon, even more people come by, and they see the trail that is now beginning to develop. They use it themselves. Eventually, what was simply a thick jungle curtain has turned into a main thoroughfare – and it has happened due solely to usage. This is exactly how our brains work. Even when it has absolutely no past experience of mastering a skill, your brain will make an attempt at it and, provided you give it enough practice, it will eventually become a default way of thinking or doing something.

3

developing good, emotionally intelligent core values

To be emotionally intelligent, you need to have or to develop a set of beliefs (or core values) on which you base your thoughts and actions. These beliefs will be personal to you and not necessarily the same as anyone else's. However, a great deal of powerful, evidence-based research has shown that there is a set of core values that transcends the passage of time, global geographical location and different religious or spiritual beliefs. These particular core values are common to emotionally intelligent people right across the world, and therefore form a good basis for developing our own idiosyncratic set of values.

In this chapter we explore these values with you and help you to select and develop those that you feel will be important in you. These core values are all components of emotionally intelligent thinking and behaviour and you will thus be well rewarded by taking time to work on them.

Developing the qualities that will increase your EI will depend somewhat on your own views of what constitutes EI qualities and values. A good place to start is to look at some of those that have been widely identified as necessary to EI. Perhaps one of the most important competencies is integrity.

Integrity

Real integrity is doing the right thing, knowing that nobody's going to know whether you did it or not.

Oprah Winfrey, broadcaster

We all like to think we have integrity, and that our actions support it. But what exactly is it?

Integrity is action based on a consistent framework of principles. A person is said to have integrity to the extent that everything they do and believe is based on the same core set of values. While those values may change, it is their consistency with each other and with your actions that determine your integrity. Those with integrity are people whose words match what they do, and what they do reflects their values. They are dependable – they don't let you down. They are 100 per cent trustworthy. Integrity is the common denominator that sustains every other value you possess.

Think about the consequences of lack of integrity. If someone promises something and does not follow through, then the individual who was counting on them and put their faith in the person's word learns mistrust. That lack of trust may extend beyond the person who broke the promise and towards others as well.

The cost of broken words

In the case of a personal relationship, the cost of a broken word is more than just the loss of trust; it includes the inflicting of deep hurt on the person who was misled.

In business, a person's word has to be good. If you cannot be true to your word, you cannot be trusted and, when that happens, how can you continue to operate in business? Integrity is important at every level and in every aspect of society.

Integrity is something that has been taught throughout history. We can find the idea and importance of integrity emphasized in many religious teachings throughout every age of humans. Integrity is more than just an idea; it is a practical and necessary character trait that is required in order to have any lasting success in this world. (Of course it is true that some people achieve success quite deliberately through a serious lack of integrity, morals and ethics. However, the danger is that it is like a house built on shifting sand, and may well crumble sooner or later.)

Having integrity is about:

* being clear about your own values
* being open about your values to others
* behaving in a way that reflects the importance of your values to you.

How to develop your integrity

Make some new rules

You may wish to make some basic 'rules' for yourself that will increase your integrity levels in the future. Here are some suggestions, and you may like to add more.

Be 100 per cent trustworthy. This does not mean always doing what others want, but it means never saying 'Yes' when you mean 'No', and it means that, once you have given your word (even in an informal way), you don't break it. It doesn't mean that you cannot get things wrong and make errors. It means owning up and apologizing sometimes, rather than covering things up and making excuses.

Never break confidentiality. If you are the possessor of information given or written with the clear understanding that you do not pass it on, don't take it upon yourself to assess the importance of keeping or breaking that undertaking. It is not for you to decide that it doesn't really matter if you tell just one person. When someone tells you a secret, keep it. If you really doubt yourself, have the integrity to ask not to be given this confidential information in the first place.

Have courage in your beliefs and be open about them. If something doesn't seem quite right to you or if you find yourself in a situation where you feel uncomfortable with what is being asked or said – say so. (You may wish to work on your assertiveness skills if you find this difficult.)

Add some further 'rules' of your own. Now add some more ideas of your own. What can you do to develop your integrity further? Write down at least three further suggestions and then start to incorporate them into your daily life.

How to develop responsibility

It simply isn't possible to be emotionally intelligent without taking responsibility for your own actions. People who fail to take responsibility say things like:

* It's not my fault I am the way I am.
* I never asked to be born.
* Life is unfair. There is no sense in trying to take control of my life.
* You can't help me, nobody can help me. I'm useless and a failure.
* When do the troubles and problems cease? I'm tired of all this.
* Life is so depressing. If only I had better luck and had been born to a healthier family, or attended a better school, or got a better job.
* How can I be responsible for what happens to me in the future? Fate, luck and other negative influences have a greater bearing on my future than I have.
* The problems in my family have influenced who I am and what I will be; there is nothing I can do to change that.
* No matter how hard I work, I will never get ahead.
* I am who I am; there is no changing me.

Has there ever been a time when you have said or thought any of the above? Don't worry if your answer is a blushing 'yes' – we are all human and go through periods of self-pity where we feel that life is against us. Just acknowledging this, understanding it and then acting to change it is all that EI asks of you.

Accepting personal responsibility includes:

* acknowledging that you are solely responsible for the choices in your life
* accepting that you are responsible for what you choose to feel or think
* accepting that you choose the direction for your life
* accepting that you cannot blame others for the choices you have made
* realizing that you determine your feelings about any events or actions addressed to you, no matter how negative they seem
* recognizing that you are your best cheerleader; it is not reasonable or healthy for you to depend on others to make you feel good about yourself
* not feeling sorry for the 'bad hand' you have been 'dealt' but taking hold of your life and giving it direction and reason
* protecting and nurturing your health and emotional well-being
* taking an honest inventory of your strengths, abilities, talents, virtues and positive points
* letting go of blame and anger towards those in your past who did the best they could, given the limitations of their knowledge, background and awareness.

How to develop openness

When we are short of self-esteem, the thought of being totally open with others is a frightening idea. A common view is that people will only like us if we hide certain aspects (many, even) of ourselves. We feel that we need to present ourselves in a certain way for others to like us, and that any sign of weakness will be harshly judged and criticized.

In reality, the opposite is true. Once we become willing to expose our weaknesses and fallibilities to others, we begin a process of true bonding. Consider for a moment who, of all your friends and acquaintances, you like the best. Those who always tell you how well things are going, how great their job is, how clever their children are, etc? I doubt it. Most likely, it will be someone who always 'says it as it is', and never tries to make anything sound either better or worse than it really is.

Exercise 5

If you normally find it difficult to reveal something about yourself that you see as a negative trait, to help you practise disclosure make a real effort to do this with someone. Do this in a social situation rather than in the workplace where it may not go down well to disclose incompetencies, and be aware of the outcome. Think about the outcome you might expect. What actually happened? What feedback did you get from the person to whom you disclosed something? In most cases, your prediction will not match what actually happens. You will probably not expect an overly positive response, but you will almost certainly get one. People will admire you for being open, they will be sympathetic if there is a problem, and they will be quick to say, 'Hey, me too, I've had that happen and I've felt that way', and there is your bonding.

Developing gratitude

We neglect gratitude as a virtue at our peril. The results of various researches show conclusively that expressing gratitude increases our sense of happiness and well-being. On a simple level gratitude can mean counting our blessings, or it can be an expression of appreciation to others that not only increases our own well-being, but theirs as well.

Psychologist Christopher Peterson has developed an exercise he calls 'Three good things'. Try this out and see how it works for you.

Exercise 6

To help you develop the value of gratitude, at the end of the day (not earlier), write down three things (no more) that went well. Also record why each event was a good one. (Peterson's rationale is that people are not especially mindful about good events unless they focus on them closely.) Most people don't notice things that are running smoothly; we usually assume that good things are our due. Accordingly, we do not think much about them and miss the potential benefits of thoughtful, conscious gratitude.

The three things on your list can be relatively small in importance: 'The postman smiled at me.' 'Someone helped me when I dropped some papers on the floor.' Or they can be large in importance: 'I just got a major promotion.' However, large things tend to illicit thanks quite easily; it is the small things that we miss and that will make a real difference. For each positive event on your list, answer in your own words the question:

Why did this good thing happen?

For example, you might consider that the postman smiled at you because you had bothered to say good morning, or simply because you consider that he finds you a nice person.

Undertake Exercise 6 for at least a week and evaluate whether there is an increase in your tendency to appreciate the small things in life – and what positive effect this has on you. Many people continue this exercise as a nightly habit. Eleanor Roosevelt was a known exponent of this, and I personally know a very happy, positive, emotionally intelligent woman who has written in her 'Golden Moments' notebook every night for 40 years.

It works!

Here are some suggestions for things you may neglect to be grateful for:

* a roof over your head
* your material possessions
* a car that runs
* your health
* your relationships
* your family
* your job
* your skills
* holidays.

When your feelings of gratitude are conditional upon temporary circumstances, such as your material possessions, your job, and your relationships, your basic character doesn't change significantly. But when you root your gratitude in something permanent, it becomes a permanent part of you. Instead of saying 'I am grateful for ...' you just say 'I am grateful.'

Developing humility

You might question the importance of humility in your quest for EI. While the dictionary defines 'humility' as, 'Modesty, lacking pretence, and not believing that you are superior to others', an ancillary definition includes: 'Having a lowly opinion of oneself, meekness.'

Bruna Martinuzzi, an EI trainer from Canada, suggests, quite correctly, that we often confuse humility with timidity. Her belief is that humility is not clothing us in an attitude of self-abasement or self-denigration. Humility is about maintaining our pride about who we are, our achievements and our worth – but without arrogance. It is the antithesis of hubris, that excessive, arrogant pride that often leads to the derailment of some, as it does with the downfall of the tragic hero in the typical Greek drama. It's about a quiet confidence without the need for an overt selling of our wares. It's about being content to let others discover the layers of our talents without having to boast about them. It's a lack of arrogance, not a lack of aggressiveness in the pursuit of achievement.

Exercise 7

Become more aware of your ability to practise humility by considering the following:

1. There are times when swallowing pride is particularly difficult, and any intentions of humility fly out the window as we become engaged in a contest of perfection, each side seeking to look good. If you find yourself in such no-win situations, consider developing some strategies to ensure that the circumstances don't lead you to lose your grace. Try this sometimes: just stop talking and allow the other person to be in the limelight. There is something very liberating in this strategy.
2. Here are three magical words that will produce more peace of mind than a week at an expensive retreat: 'You are right.'
3. Catch yourself if you benignly slip into preaching or coaching without permission – is zeal to impose your point of view overtaking discretion? Is your correction of others reflective of your own needs?
4. Seek others' input on how you are getting on in your leadership path. Ask: 'How am I doing?' It takes humility to ask such a question. And even more humility to consider the answer.
5. Encourage the practice of humility through your own example: every time you share credit for successes with others, you reinforce this ethos for others.

Source: Adapted from Bruna Martinuzzi, *Optimism: The Hidden Asset* (2006)

Developing courage

Courage takes many forms, and so it is different for each of us. I saw it last month in an old school friend who had to deal with his mother's death two weeks before Christmas. There are also sisters of two friends who win awards for courage from me: one because when chemotherapy made her bald, she still kept her promise to volunteer at her daughter's school. She wore neither a wig nor a baseball cap; she carried a determination to show that life goes on. The other friend's sister has multiple sclerosis. I've lost count of the treatments she's agreed to try because, among other reasons, she wants to dance with her husband again. Do you think they consider themselves courageous? I doubt it. But they are, as all of us are every morning we get up. Every time we drive on the motorway or fly in an aeroplane, every time we say 'yes', or say 'no'. It takes courage to walk into a room full of strangers, to give a speech, to have a baby, or to have none at all. It takes courage to fall in love, to learn a language, to hug like you mean it, to say goodbye.

In an emotionally intelligent life, the opposite of courage isn't fear. It's complacency. 'Oh, well,' we think. 'We've always smoked, why stop now?' Or we've thought about exercising, but our grandparents lived to be 90, so why do we need to sweat? We need to because life isn't about resting on our laurels or succumbing to our habits. It's about doing something that will make us better people – physically, mentally, emotionally – for ourselves and for those who love us.

> ***Moral excellence comes about as a result of habit. We become just by doing just acts, temperate by doing temperate acts, courageous by doing courageous acts.***
>
> Aristotle, Greek philosopher

Developing motivation

While integrity is the driver of other emotionally intelligent values, self-motivation is the driver of achieving these to the best of your abilities. Motives are what cause us to act – otherwise, why bother?

Why you need motivation

* You cannot always rely on others to encourage you. If you have positive friends who are always there when you need them then you are indeed lucky but you cannot always count on this. Often, when you face any difficulties in

your life you must rely on your own motivation to get you through.

* You need self-motivation to achieve your goals. This is what gives you the ability to encourage yourself to accept opportunities and challenges.
* You need self-motivation to plan and find a broader direction in your life.

In order to motivate yourself, you must give more significance to your thinking, feeling and behaviour. This brings us back to the notion of personal awareness.

* Learn to think positively by seeking the positive aspects of a situation before considering the alternatives.
* Learn to recognize which of your feelings are emotional, which are physiological and which are intuitive.
* Instead of asking, 'Why has this happened?' ask, 'What can I do to change it?'

As you learn new strategies for improving your EI, remember that practice makes perfect. You won't increase your EI simply by deciding to do things differently. Practice is what will strengthen the pathway between your emotions and your reason. Repetition of new, more emotionally intelligent behaviours will increase your motivation to acquire skills that are lasting and enduring, rather than transient.

4

how resilience improves your emotional intelligence

'I simply can't bear it'. 'I won't be able to cope with that'. These and similar phrases can often be heard on the lips of those who lack the quality of resilience. Emotionally intelligent people possess resilience, so the two go hand in hand. As you become more emotionally intelligent, you will become more resilient, and vice versa. Resilience means, in essence, being able to respond in a positive way to difficult and upsetting emotions. It means standing firm in the face of adversity rather than running away and it means the cultivation of an acceptance of setbacks so that you can move on in spite of them, rather than seeing them as impenetrable roadblocks.

This chapter will teach you more about the importance of resilience in an emotionally intelligent and successful life. You will discover its characteristics and how to develop and integrate these into your life and you will find that you already have all the resources within you to develop resilience that you perhaps simply didn't know were there.

How resilient are you?

When something goes wrong, do you bounce back or do you fall apart? People with resilience harness inner strengths and tend to rebound more quickly from a setback or challenge, whether it's a job loss, an illness or the death of a loved one. To be resilient, you must also be emotionally intelligent, and to be emotionally intelligent, you must be resilient.

In contrast, people who are less resilient – with lower levels of EI – may dwell on problems, feel victimized, become overwhelmed and turn to unhealthy coping mechanisms, such as substance abuse. They may even be more inclined to develop mental health problems. While resilience won't necessarily make your problems go away, it can give you the ability to see past them, find some enjoyment in life and handle things better.

Here are some definitions of resilience, as it has been defined by a variety of researchers in the field:

* 'Remaining competent despite exposure to misfortune or stressful events.'
* 'A capacity that allows a person to prevent, minimize or overcome the damaging effects of adversity.'
* 'The capacity some people have to adapt successfully despite exposure to severe stressors.'
* 'The human capacity to face, overcome and even be strengthened by the adversities of life.'
* 'The process of, capacity for, or outcome of successful adaptation despite challenging or threatening circumstances.'

Understand what having good resilience can give you

Resilience means using your emotions to adapt to stress and adversity

Resilience is the ability to adapt well to stress, adversity, trauma or tragedy. It means that, overall, you remain stable and maintain healthy levels of psychological and physical functioning in the face of disruption or chaos.

Resilience helps you to cope with temporary disruptions in your life and the challenges they throw up. For instance, you may have a period when you worry about an elderly parent who is sick. Resilience ensures that, despite your concerns, you're able to continue with daily tasks and remain generally optimistic about life.

EI is vital in enhancing resilience because it means more than merely trying to weather a storm. It doesn't mean you ignore feelings of sadness over a loss – it actually means, in EI terms, becoming *more* aware of them, and then being able to deal with them. It does not mean that you always have to be strong and that you can't ask others for support – in fact, reaching out to others is a key component of nurturing resilience in yourself.

* Resilience doesn't mean that you're unable to express your emotions or that you don't feel them.
* Resilience can provide protection against emotional disorders such as depression and anxiety. It will help individuals deal constructively with the after-effects of trauma.
* Resilience may even help strengthen you against certain physical illnesses such as heart disease and diabetes.
* People who are resilient have the ability to say to themselves: 'This disaster has occurred, but I have a choice. I can either dwell on it or I can do something about it.'

Resilience gives you the skills to endure hardship

Resilience can help you to endure loss, stress, traumas and other challenges. It will enable you to develop many internal resources that you can draw upon to help you survive challenges and to thrive in the midst of chaos and hardship.

Exercise 8

Here is a test to measure your resiliency – your ability to bounce back from stressful situations. It is based on discovering the level of characteristics you possess that make people more resilient. For example, flexibility, self-confidence, creativity and an ability to learn from experience.

Look at each statement below, and note down the number (from 1 to 5) that most closely describes how much you agree with it.

1 = strongly disagree; 5 = strongly agree

1 I don't allow difficulties to get me down for long. ☐

2 I am able to be open about my feelings; I don't harbour grievances and I don't get downhearted easily. ☐

3 I am normally confident and possess good self-esteem. ☐

4 If things go wrong, I am able to stay calm and work out the best course of action. ☐

5 I'm optimistic that any difficulties presented are temporary and I expect to overcome them. ☐

6 I usually adapt to changes in circumstances quickly and without fuss. ☐

7 My positive emotions are strong enough to help me move on from setbacks. ☐

8 I can be quite creative in thinking up solutions to problems. ☐

9 I normally trust my intuition and it usually serves me well. ☐

10 I am curious, ask questions and I am keen to know how things work. ☐

11 I am generally at ease with myself. ☐

12 I'm a good problem solver and enjoy the challenges that problems present. ☐

13 I can usually find something to laugh about, even in the direst situations. ☐

14 I am able to be self-effacing and laugh at myself. ☐
15 I always try to find something positive to learn from my experiences. ☐
16 I'm usually good at understanding other people's feelings. ☐
17 I am flexible, and can usually adapt fairly quickly to situations as they change. ☐
18 I try to look ahead and anticipate and, if possible, deflect problems before they happen. ☐
19 I usually consider myself to be strong and independent, and I don't tend to give in when things are difficult. ☐
20 I'm open-minded about other people's views and lifestyles. ☐
21 I am not constantly anxious when things are uncertain. ☐
22 I don't usually fail at tasks I am presented with, provided they are reasonably within my capabilities. ☐
23 I regard myself, and believe others regard me, as a good leader. ☐
24 I believe that experiencing difficult situations can make me stronger. ☐
25 I believe that something good comes out of every bad thing. ☐

Scores

100–125 You are extremely resilient.
76–99 You normally bounce back quite well.
50–75 You can deal with certain things, but find others beyond you.
Under 50 You find recovery from difficulties hard and you need to develop your personal strength to deal with what life throws at you.

Here are some suggestions for improving your resilience that you may find helpful.

* Look back at other times in your life when you have had to cope with difficulties – perhaps something you

felt you would not be able to overcome. What actually happened? What helped you to resolve the situation? Was there anything that didn't help? If so, ensure that you don't repeat that mistake. Building on the way you coped well with previous difficult situations will increase your resilience when you are faced with a new problem. Think also about how you may have changed as a result of dealing with the difficulty. Reflect on this. Are you perhaps stronger than you thought? If you really don't think so – if you feel worse as a result of your experiences – then consider what changes you might make to improve things next time.

* Build strong, positive relationships with your family and friends. These relationships provide mutual support in times of difficulty, which will help your own resilience and help you to offer this to others. Becoming involved in groups and/or charity work is also helpful. The power of the group, both to nurture you and give you support, is enormous. Groups also ensure that you will never feel alone during tough times.
* Use your thought-challenging skills. Even when things seem quite dire, constantly ask yourself whether there is a more positive way that you can look at things. If you can encourage yourself to remain hopeful and optimistic when you're in the middle of a crisis, it will be much easier to get through. Resilience is not always about putting things right, but about taking an optimistic view even when you cannot change events.
* When you can, trying to find the funny side of things will always strengthen you – as well as relaxing you in a tense situation. Of course, this is sometimes extremely hard, but seeing the funny side doesn't mean you are not taking things seriously – it simply means that when emotions come to the fore, positive emotions will keep you stronger than negative ones.

The idea that being angry and distressed is somehow more helpful than being good-humoured is, of course, unfounded.

* Never forget the basics. Your personal ability to develop resilience will depend a great deal on looking after yourself. Make sure that your diet is healthy, you exercise regularly, perhaps practise relaxation exercises or take a yoga class, take care of your appearance and make plenty of time for activities that you enjoy. Nurturing your mind and body in this way will keep you mentally, as well as physically, strong. Having a sense of personal well-being strengthens your belief that you can tackle difficulties and overcome them.
* Develop a philosophy of acceptance. Be flexible. Few things stay the same, and it is often hard to anticipate changes that may affect your life – sometimes quite drastically. If you can be open-minded about life events, you will upset yourself less and you will have far more energy to face and, if necessary, tackle changes. You will adapt more easily and see the positive side of new events, rather than grieving for what has passed.
* Do something every day that gives you a sense of accomplishment and achievement. This may be something you really don't want to do for a variety of reasons, but pushing yourself to face up to it and get on with it will strengthen you and make you feel good. Get into a regular habit. Don't discourage yourself by focusing on tasks that seem unachievable. Instead, ask yourself, 'What's one thing I know I can accomplish today that helps me move in the direction I want to go?'
* With chronic problems, stop wishing and hoping that they will go away, and take some action to put them right. Many of us spend a great deal of time and energy on simply wishing things would change. Wishing that your problems

will go away doesn't usually work and wastes a lot of valuable time when you could be actually doing something about them. Take decisive action rather than detaching yourself from problems and stresses. Once you address your problems with an action plan, you are on the way to overcoming them.

* Be proud of yourself. Think in positive terms about your abilities and strengths, and mentally encourage yourself to face problems with confidence. Believe you can do it. Positive self-talk is often brushed aside as meaning little – in fact it is a very powerful tool. The more you tell yourself that you are capable and strong, that you can withstand difficulties and criticism, the more control you will have over events and situations in your life and confidence in your ability to manage them well.
* Everything is relative. Sometimes we see our problems in isolation rather than against the bigger picture of the world around us. This can negatively discourage us as we may see our difficulties as acute and overwhelming. Look around you and evaluate your problems against those of the wider world – and perhaps even against those you have weathered before. Once you get a better perspective, your problem will become easier to resolve.

Learn the factors in resilience

A combination of factors contributes to resilience. As stated earlier, it is not one individual attribute, but a process involving both internal cognitive and personality factors and the development of external, helpfully protective factors such as a supporting family. Relationships that create love and trust, provide role models, and offer encouragement and reassurance help bolster your resilience.

Resilience helps your confidence and management of emotions

Several additional factors are associated with resilience, including:

* the capacity to make realistic plans and take steps to carry them out
* a positive view of yourself and confidence in your strengths and abilities
* skills in communication and problem solving
* the capacity to manage strong feelings and impulses.

All of these are factors that people can develop within themselves. Now think about your personal strategies for building resilience to manage your emotions. Developing resilience is a personal journey. People do not all react in the same way to traumatic and stressful life events. An approach to building resilience that works for one person might not work for another; people use varying strategies. Some variations may reflect cultural differences, as a person's culture might impact on how they communicate feelings and deal with adversity – for example, whether and how a person connects with significant others, including extended family members and community resources. With growing cultural diversity, the public has greater access to a number of different approaches to building resilience.

5

anger: our strongest emotion and how emotional intelligence defeats it

Managing our emotions can take time and hard work. Managing our anger can present us with the greatest challenge of all and can often seem just too difficult. 'I simply lost it'. 'It was all too much'. 'I was so angry I couldn't think straight'. Such phrases are often uttered not only by aggressive bullies but also by otherwise decent and caring people. So can we be both emotionally intelligent and angry? Yes, we can. We are not talking about eliminating anger altogether but keeping personal control over it, so that we use it effectively and appropriately – to fight for injustice, for example, when our anger will hopefully produce positive results for those less able to fight for themselves.

This chapter will help you learn to discriminate between healthy and unhealthy anger and to replace unhealthy anger with more constructive ways of dealing with difficult situations and achieving your aims. It will teach you to manage your anger in an emotionally intelligent way.

When managing our emotions seems too hard

> ***Anybody can become angry, that is easy, but to be angry with the right person, and to the right degree, and at the right time, and for the right purpose, and in the right way: that is not within everybody's power, that is not easy.***
>
> Aristotle, Greek philosopher

Emotional intelligence is all about being aware of our emotions, identifying them and then controlling them. But what if we can't? What if, no matter how many books we read and seminars we attend, when push comes to shove, the moment we find ourselves riled, the emotional brain takes over and we 'lose it'?

I work with many clients who are good, decent, caring people. Yet anger seems to be the one emotion that they cannot control. This 'anger habit' includes the tendency to experience temper tantrums, feelings of ongoing frustration, resentment and irritability. Of all the emotions, with the exception of passionate love, anger seems to be the hardest to control.

Can you be emotionally intelligent if you cannot control your anger? We all know people who have the kindest of hearts, and who are emotionally very open, yet their one obvious weakness is that they get angry very quickly.

High anger can ruin both personal and professional relationships, as well as be detrimental to your health. At its worst, anger can also kill. Road rage is an example of this. An otherwise rational man or woman becomes so angry with another driver's behaviour that they decide to get their own back by giving chase. An accident results that kills two of the people involved. There may have been many reasons for this crazy, destructive behaviour – too much to do, setting off late, not allowing enough time to get from A to B, generally feeling that people are inconsiderate – but it was the inability to manage the emotion of high anger that resulted in the tragedy.

Twenty-first century intolerance

We are more concerned than ever with our rights (fuelled, very often, by a compensation culture). We are less philosophical, less inclined to 'put things down to experience'. If our demands are not now met in a way that we have come to expect, we become angry. As we become generally angrier – so do others. This means it takes a lot less for us to get into a fight with someone, or to be provoked ourselves.

Suppressing anger

Expressing anger, especially in the workplace, is becoming less and less acceptable. This means that by expressing anger inappropriately we may risk our job, or at least disciplinary action. We might be sued by someone who feels that we have exhibited aggression towards them. We therefore often bottle up anger, instead of dealing with it, and this can be exceedingly harmful to both our emotional and physical well-being.

If you do not wish to be prone to anger, do not feed the habit; give it nothing which may tend to its increase.

Epictetus (AD 55–135)

Me? Angry?

We all have different views on what is acceptable and what is not when it comes to anger. What may seem an angry response to person A is a natural way of dealing with situations for person B.

Exercise 9

Are you aware of your own anger? Answer the following questions to check it out. Score your answers: 0 = never, 1 = occasionally, 2 = often.

1. Others comment on my aggressive responses.
2. Waiting in queues drives me mad.
3. I can't tolerate rudeness.
4. I always respond badly to criticism.
5. I start arguments easily.
6. Driving in traffic causes me huge stress.
7. I consider most other drivers on the road to be bad drivers.
8. I find most shop assistants and helplines, etc. quite incompetent.
9. In difficult discussions with people, I tend to get angry the most quickly.
10. I let petty annoyances really work me up.

Scores

0–7: Don't worry; you stay well balanced in most tricky situations.

8–14: You are responding to stressful situations with anger too often.

15–20: Your angry responses may cause some serious damage if you don't make urgent changes.

If you scored highly in Exercise 9, don't worry – you can make changes to calm down your anger. Simply accepting the reality that you do get inappropriately angry is half the battle to reducing such responses.

The word 'inappropriate' is important here. Anger is not always a bad thing. It can often be emotionally intelligent to get angry. The key to this is being able to *control* your anger, and to use it only when it is appropriate, while containing it when it is not.

When is anger good?

Exercise 10

What would you say the differences are between healthy, constructive, emotionally intelligent anger and unhealthy, destructive anger?

Have you ever thought of anger as being a good, emotionally intelligent thing? If not, think about it for a moment, and write down three or four suggestions as to when it might be.

Let's take a look at some possibilities of anger as a good, emotionally intelligent action.

Anger at injustice

You see someone kicking a dog, hear on the news that innocent people in a far off country are being brutally treated, notice someone at work who is always unfairly picked on by the boss ... These are situations where injustice prevails, and we need to get angry about these things. World starvation, unnecessary wars, people dying through lack of health care – the only way to get anything done about such situations is for at least some of us to feel very angry about them.

Anger to get results

As an absolutely last resort, if you really need to get results from recalcitrant staff, motor mechanics, waiters, your children, etc. then reasonable anger can work a treat.

Anger as a motivational tool

When you finally hear yourself (or someone else) say 'Right. That's it. I'm not taking any more of this', you know that you (or they) are going to blow your top in order to get some action. In a sense, you are bringing some energy to the situation.

Anger as a release

'Letting it all out' has actually been shown to have health benefits, compared to repressed anger that we hold inside and which eats away at us. However, there are ways of letting things out that don't involve becoming apoplectic, so use this release with caution.

Anger as an alert signal

Healthy anger can let you know that something is wrong. You can use this alert to work out what is worrying you, and then do something positive to change it. For example, if you find yourself becoming irritated every time you need to meet with a particular work colleague, ask yourself why they annoy you so. It may be that they are always late for your meetings, always dominate the discussion or regularly cancel at the last minute. Becoming aware of your anger in these circumstances encourages you to change the situation so that it is less stressful.

The point of taking a look at healthy anger is to bring home to you that you do not need to eliminate this emotion from your life. Anger can be a good emotion, but in appropriate circumstances. Inappropriate anger is a problem.

Exercise 11

To help discover whether your own anger is healthy or not, think of two or three situations in which you became angry in the last week or so. Now think for a moment about the outcome. Do you feel that, in any of these instances, your anger had achieved a good result? If so, what was it? Do you feel that your anger was an emotionally intelligent response in these circumstances?

Where anger comes from

Anger stems from our expectations regarding the ideals and behaviours of others. We expect people to treat us fairly and they don't. We expect them to be nice to us and they aren't. We expect them to help us and they walk away.

Each time someone breaks a rule of ours, violates a contract or acts against our wishes, a possible option is to react with anger. We do not absolutely have to – it is our choice. Unfortunately, we do not always feel that we are in control of this choice – we feel unable to manage our emotions and it is as though it has already been decided for us and we act accordingly.

Earlier in this book (see Chapter 4), we did a lot of work on emotionally intelligent thinking. You now need to use the skills you have learned to help you to manage and reduce your angry thoughts and feelings.

The anger spiral

You are familiar now with the relationship between what we think and how we feel. A situation such as a rude boss may be the external trigger and our thought, 'How dare he speak to me like that?', triggers the emotion of anger. It is the thought that drives the emotion – at least initially. However, once in the spiral, the emotion then drives further negative thoughts, such as, 'He really is a bully. He shouldn't be allowed to get away with it.' In turn, this makes you even angrier than before, and so on, until the anger gets quite out of control. Where you lack the ability to manage your anger, this can create an extremely dangerous situation in many ways.

Have you recently found yourself in an anger spiral? Think about your emotions at the start of the situation, the middle and the end of the situation. Did your anger increase in the way we have described above as your thinking became more negative? How long did it take for your anger to go down? Were you able to do anything positive to calm yourself?

Let's take a look at someone who gets into an anger spiral and learn from his mistakes. We'll use thought challenging as our tool to see how we can help our guinea pig reduce his angry thoughts and responses.

Our guinea pig

Neil is a 35-year-old computer specialist. He works in a high pressure job, feels stressed most of the time and is perpetually offended at myriad slights and abuses. He is highly competitive and takes absolutely nothing lightly. In his mind, others are just out to annoy him, make his life difficult and increase his stress levels – an indifferent shop assistant, a slow driver ahead of him, a leisurely bank clerk – any of these things can trigger his rage.

To help Neil, we're going to break his pattern of anger down into a series of steps. Each step represents a 'choice point'. Neil can choose to intervene at each step, cool down and break the pattern, or he can continue along his destructive path.

Exercise 12

To help you learn how to get out of your own anger spiral, read Neil's difficulties and see if you can work out in advance what he could do to get out of his anger spiral – where his 'choice point' is (remember, these are choice points that you also always have – learn to identify them). What would you do if you were him, and what can you learn from what happens?

The 'should' rule

As we mentioned earlier, much of our anger is based on the premise that others 'should' think and act the way we do. They should share our values and behave as we believe that they 'should'. An important step in getting rid of angry emotions consists of breaking the 'should' rule.

Much of Neil's life is governed by such rules. He has rules and expectations for his own behaviour, for others' behaviour and even feels the weight of others' rules on him. He has more rules than a legal tome. The result? Anger, guilt and intense pressure to live up to his standards.

Yet Neil cannot live up to such unrelenting standards, and neither can others (and neither can you). Neil demands, 'People should listen to me.' 'They should stay out of the way.' 'I should have total control over this situation.' But the fact of the matter is that people don't listen, they do get in his way and he cannot control their behaviour. At this point, Neil has the choice to accept the circumstances that have arisen or battle away against reality, demanding that it should not be that way. It would be much more preferable if he were listened to and left alone, but he cannot demand it.

Exercise 13

Neil has an option to challenge the 'should' style of thinking that is causing him to get so angry.

What could Neil say instead of the thoughts he has? Based on the work you have already done on the link between thoughts and emotions, write a short script for Neil. Then check below to see if you are thinking along the right lines.

For the first step, here are some anger reducing thoughts for Neil.

* 'The fact of the matter is that people do ignore my wishes and intrude. What, constructively, can I do when that happens?'
* 'I can continue to follow my own "rules", to treat others fairly and well, but not insist that they respond to me in the same way. It would be nice if they did, but if they don't, then they don't.'
* 'I need to stop disturbing myself about something I can do nothing about.'

Exercise 14

This will help you banish your own 'shoulds'. Do you have 'should' rules for how others should behave? Write a few of them down. For example, 'People should not drop litter in the street.'

Now rewrite these sentences without using the word 'should'. This may be quite hard to do for some of the rules in which you believe strongly. However, it will help you to begin to think more flexibly and to reduce the anger you feel when people ignore the rules that are important to you.

Coming to terms with the idea that others might not follow our own ideas about behaviour is a good start.

Some other tools to calm down angry situations

As the second step, work out what's *really* upsetting you. Examine what really hurts when one of your rules is broken. For example, when Neil is angry and hurt, he can ask himself, 'What really hurts here?' Maybe he thinks, 'People are rude and insensitive', 'I'll be made the victim', or 'I'm powerless to do anything about this.' What hurts the most is Neil's inability to change people's behaviour.

Exercise 15

What could Neil say instead of the thoughts he has above? As you did previously, write a short script for Neil. Then check your suggestions against ours below.

As the third step, here is how Neil might calm himself:

* 'There is no evidence that I should be able to control people.'
* 'People are responsible for their own beliefs, behaviours, attitudes and assumptions.'
* 'Perhaps I can see myself not as a victim, but as a person who can choose how to be.'

Neil can respond to hot, anger-driven thoughts with cooler, more level-headed thoughts.

* Neil initially thinks, 'How dare he?' but he can replace that thought with, 'He thinks he is trying to help me.'
* Neil thinks, 'How stupid can she be?' but he can instead respond, 'She's human.'

Exercise 16

This will help you change your script. Who or what annoyed you the most in the last couple of days? Recall how angry you felt, and what you were thinking.

Using any of the tools we've discussed so far in this chapter, change the script. How angry do you think these alternative thoughts would make you?

Using relaxation skills

The fourth step is to respond to angry feelings themselves. Neil can do this by practising relaxation and deep breathing. He can relax his muscles and refocus his attention away from the stressful situation. Learn to do this yourself.

When your emotions take over, your body reacts by increasing your heart rate in order to move blood very quickly around the body. This, in turn, causes your breathing to become shallow and quick. To reduce your anger, your task is to reduce your heart rate and breathing to a point where your body is able to relax at will.

You can use breathing and muscle relaxation together for maximum effect. Try both, and see if either suits you better, or if a combination of the two is the most ideal.

Deep breathing

Learning to control your breathing is actually a big step towards controlling many of your 'high' emotions. Becoming physically relaxed calms down our brains, which prevents our emotional mind from dominating the proceedings. If you learn this simple skill, and practise it regularly, you will be well on the way to managing your anger.

Firstly, start noticing how you breathe.

* Find some space somewhere and lie on the floor on your back, with your knees slightly bent, in a relaxed position.
* Place your right hand on your stomach, just where your waistline is.
* Place your left hand in the centre of your chest.
* Now, without changing your natural rhythm, simply breathe in and out, and look out for the hand that rises highest when you breathe in – is it your right hand (on your stomach) or your left hand (on your chest)?

This will tell you, in simple terms, whether you are a deep breather (when the hand on your stomach lifts the highest) – or a shallow breather (when the hand on your chest rises higher). The chances are that if anger is a problem for you, you will be a naturally shallow breather.

Exercises to improve your breathing

You are seeking to 'feel' your breathing relax your body – and you will know when this happens. Experts may tell you, 'Count to four', 'Count to six', 'Count to eight' when you breathe. This may be confusing and it can lead some people to hyperventilate. Instead, find a count that suits the length of your breath and within which you can feel a rhythm that is comfortable and breathing that is slow and deep. Whatever works for you is fine.

Horizontal or vertical? Another option, which you should decide for yourself, is whether you sit down or lie down. You can lie down if you prefer. However, bear in mind that the goal is for you to be able use this skill 'whenever and wherever', and so sitting, or even standing, will be a better option.

1 Place your hands on your stomach and chest, as you did before. (While this is good for practising, if you use deep breathing away from home or in a crisis situation, simply imagine this part.)

2. Now breathe in slowly through your nose (if you want to count to, say four, please do).
3. Ensure as you do this that the hand on your stomach rises, and the hand on your chest remains as unmoving as possible.
4. Now exhale slowly (count again if this helps you) and, as you do, feel the hand on your stomach gently fall back.

This is a simple breathing technique that you can use whenever you like.

Muscle relaxation for calming emotion

A surprising, quick and easy calming trick is yawning. We tend to think yawning simply indicates tiredness or boredom, but on many occasions it is actually helping to calm us down. Yawning ensures more oxygen enters our lungs and moves into our bloodstream, de-tensing muscles and de-stressing our brains. So if you feel a yawn coming on, and you have enough privacy, don't stifle it – use it as the ultra deep breath that it is and let it flow right through you.

To begin with, practise all of the exercises, and you will soon find that some seem to work for you better than others. If this is the case, select only those exercises to practise, and eventually reduce these to just one or two. You will have these exercises 'at the ready' when your emotions appear to need some extra management help.

Make sure you are in a setting that is quiet and comfortable. You can choose whether to sit in a chair or lie down – most exercises lend themselves equally well to either. Take a few slow, deep breaths before you start. Then tense each muscle group hard for about 10 seconds and let go of it suddenly, enjoying the sensation of limpness. Allow the relaxation to develop for at least 15–20 seconds before going on to the next group of muscles. Notice how the muscle group feels when relaxed, in contrast to how it felt when tensed, before going on to the next group of muscles. You might also say to yourself 'relax' as you do so. Here are the 16 exercises.

* Clench your fists. Hold for 10 seconds and then release for about 15–20 seconds.

* Tighten your biceps muscles by drawing your forearms up towards your shoulders and 'making a muscle' with both arms. Hold for about 10 seconds and then relax for 15–20 seconds.
* Tighten your triceps – the muscles on the undersides of your upper arms – by extending your arms out straight and locking your elbows. Hold, then relax.
* Tighten your forehead muscles by raising your eyebrows as high as you can. Hold for about 10 seconds and then relax for 15–20 seconds.
* Tighten your jaws by opening your mouth so widely that you stretch the muscles around the hinges of your jaw. Hold, then relax. Let your lips part and let your jaw hang loose.
* Tighten up the muscles around your eyes by clenching them tightly shut. Hold for about 10 seconds and then relax for 15–20 seconds. Imagine sensations of deep relaxation spreading all around the area of your eyes.
* Tighten the muscles in the back of your neck by gently pulling your head way back, as if you were going to touch your head to your back. Focus only on tensing the muscles in your neck. Hold for about 10 seconds and then relax for 15–20 seconds. Repeat this step if your neck feels especially tight.
* If you are lying down, take a few deep breaths and tune in to the weight of your head sinking into whatever surface it is resting on.
* Tighten your shoulders by raising them up as if you were going to touch your ears. Hold for about 10 seconds and then relax for 15–20 seconds.
* Tighten the muscles around your shoulder blades by pushing your shoulder blades back as if you were going to touch them together. Hold the tension in your shoulder blades for about 10 seconds, and then relax for 15–20 seconds. Repeat this step if your upper back feels especially tight.

* Tighten the muscles of your chest by taking a deep breath. Hold for up to 10 seconds and then release slowly. Imagine any excess tension flowing away with the exhalation.
* Tighten your stomach muscles by sucking your stomach in. Hold and then release. Imagine a wave of relaxation spreading through your abdomen.
* Tighten your lower back by arching it up. (You should omit this exercise if you have lower back pain.) Hold, then relax.
* Tighten your buttocks by pulling them together. Hold, then relax. Imagine the muscles in your hips going loose and limp.
* Squeeze the muscles of your thighs all the way down to your knees. You will probably have to tighten your hips along with your thighs, since the thigh muscles attach at the pelvis. Hold and then relax. Feel your thigh muscles smoothing out and relaxing completely.
* Tighten your feet by curling all of your toes downward. Hold, then relax.

Now imagine a wave of relaxation slowly spreading throughout your body, starting at your head and gradually penetrating every muscle group all the way down to your toes.

Prevent stress and anger from making us act spitefully

As a fifth step to reducing his anger, Neil needs to look at how he gives himself permission to think in a thoroughly spiteful way. These thoughts allow Neil to treat others in ways that he himself would not want to be treated. 'He deserved it.' 'I just want her to hurt the way I have been hurt.' 'This is the only way I can get my point across.' Neil needs to recognize these ideas as con artistry. They con him into throwing aside his morals and engaging in threats, sarcasm and demands. Neil must remind himself of the costs of such strategies, and the benefits of remaining calm and fair.

Control aggressive behaviour

The sixth step is to look at the aggressive behaviour that comes from angry thinking. Neil gives himself permission to act aggressively and ignore the rights of other people. Imagine Neil getting worked up with a sales assistant who is interminably slow. He starts speaking loudly and rudely, and demanding to see the manager. The assistant then gets angry back and a row ensues. What other choices does Neil have?

* He could attempt to understand the cause of the assistant's slowness.
* He could put himself in the assistant's shoes, imagine what they are thinking and feeling, and attempt to understand their point of view.
* He could ask himself how important the delay really is.

This will help to:

* decrease Neil's anger
* decrease the assistant's anger
* increase the likelihood that the assistant will hear what Neil has to say
* increase the likelihood of Neil and the assistant having a rational and reasonable conversation.

Learning to own your anger

One of the difficulties of managing our emotions in difficult situations is the idea that none of this is our fault. If the other person had not done this, that or the other, we would never have reacted in that way. Actually, you may be partially right. Someone may have been extremely thoughtless, careless, acted stupidly or whatever, and you may be the victim of their rotten judgement. However, while the other person is responsible for their actions, you are equally responsible for your response.

* You are the owner of your anger.
* You are the decision maker and decide when and to what extent you use this emotion.
* No one else decides this for you.
* Of course, people sometimes work very hard to provoke you. Nonetheless, managing your anger in an emotionally intelligent way is still your responsibility. You control – and therefore decide on – your reactions.

Usually when people are sad, they don't do anything. They just cry over their condition. But when they get angry, they bring about change.

Malcolm X, political activist and speaker

Reducing angry emotions with humour

Using humour is an excellent tool for defusing anger. It can help you gain a more balanced perspective and help you find the funny side. For example, if you have spent the entire afternoon putting together a flat-pack bookcase, and as you stand back to admire it, it falls apart, you can either get furious or laugh. Try laughter. This will take a lot of the edge off your fury, and humour can always be relied on to help relax a tense situation.

6

emotional intelligence and others: developing social responsibility

We have, so far, focused on emotionally intelligent self awareness. Now we are going to look at what we might call 'Other awareness'. This means extending our emotional intelligence from understanding ourselves to understanding others. To achieve this we need to develop qualities such as empathy, open mindedness and forgiveness. Empathy allows us to step into someone else's shoes and see the world through their eyes. Open mindedness enables us to appreciate and support the views of others even when we don't agree with their views ourselves. Forgiveness enables us to move forwards positively and develop relationships rather than harbour grievances that stunt them. Brought together, these qualities give us a sense of good social responsibility that will be of benefit not only to ourselves but in this case, more importantly, to others.

This chapter will teach you how to achieve this.

Developing empathy and understanding

Empathy is commonly defined as an ability to recognize, perceive and directly feel the emotion of another. It is often characterized as the ability to 'put oneself into another's shoes' or to experience the outlook or emotions of another within oneself.

Empathy is arguably the basic building block for positive relationships. It also encourages motivation. We are far more likely to act on someone else's behalf, to help them out and support them, if we can feel and appreciate their emotions.

Learning to understand someone else's point of view

We can never truly know what another person feels – and it would be impertinent to assume that we could – but in order to connect closely with others, we need to be able to appreciate at least something of their perspective. We can often achieve this in the simplest and most straightforward way by expressing to another person what we understand to be the emotions they are feeling. This allows the other person to feel heard and understood. You need never worry if you are wrong, as the other person can simply correct you with 'No, I wasn't quite feeling that, I was feeling this ...' and this will help you to fully understand, rather than make an assumption that might be wrong.

Learning to develop empathy

The qualities of empathetic people are that:

* they have close, intimate relationships with others
* they are able to communicate clearly and openly with most people
* they have a genuine interest in the concerns and difficulties of other people
* they are able to appreciate someone else's point of view, even when they don't personally agree with it
* they are able to forgive without rancour.

Empathy is very powerful. Each time you use it to show understanding of a tense or antagonistic encounter, you shift the balance. An argumentative and difficult exchange becomes a more collaborative alliance. When you achieve this, you increase your ability to move to a satisfactory outcome for all concerned. No one, after all, is going to give you what you desire if they feel misunderstood or under attack. When you express an understanding of their position, they feel heard and understood. The emotional bond between you strengthens, and the other person is more inclined to work with you, not against you.

Misconceptions about empathy

Don't confuse empathy with sympathy. Sympathy – while a valid emotion – is more concerned with your personal view of events. It is an 'If I were you ...' statement, suggesting that you would feel sorry for the other person's dilemma if you were in it. Empathy shows an understanding of the emotions that the other person might be feeling. Sympathy can sometimes be described as 'colluding' – 'Oh, how dreadful', 'Oh, poor you' – whereas empathy expresses an understanding of the other person's position even where you don't feel sympathy for it.

Empathy isn't agreeing or approving. It is acknowledging an understanding. You may totally disapprove of another person's actions, but you may also understand their own need to act in that particular way.

When empathy disappears

One of the hardest challenges of developing empathy is that it tends to fall by the wayside when we need it most. This is when emotional intelligence will come to your aid. When we are under stress, feeling misunderstood, irritated or on the defensive, we can easily let our emotions rule the day. We respond without thinking, and can appear insensitive or resentful.

This takes us back to the work we did on self-awareness in chapters 1–5. You can use this to gauge your emotions – your mounting irritation, for example – and contain your impulses and act sensibly in the face of provocation.

Using EI skills will enable you to call upon your empathetic side in order to understand the other person's position.

Insight

Make it a rule always to express to another person what you perceive to be their point of view before you tell them your own and you will be developing empathy. In other words, let someone else feel heard and understood before you say, 'Now let me tell you how I view this.'

Exercise 17

To help you develop your empathy, for the next week practise being 'open-minded'. Empathy requires genuineness, and open-mindedness is the key to this genuineness. Whenever someone makes a statement that you strongly disagree with, rather than simply launching in with your alternative views, practise seeing their point of view by saying something like:

* 'That sounds like you think ...'

Or:

* 'You obviously feel very strongly that ...'

There is nothing wrong with disagreeing with someone, but being open-minded means that you don't invalidate their view – you have respect for it, and appreciate that the way you feel is only a point of view, as well.

Learning to take responsibility

Responsibility: a detachable burden easily shifted to the shoulders of God, Fate, Fortune, Luck or one's neighbour. In the days of astrology it was customary to unload it upon a star.

Ambrose Bierce, *The Devil's Dictionary*, 1911

Often, one of the most difficult things to do is to take responsibility for the mistakes we make in life, especially in relationships with others. This is because it is very hard to admit that we, and not the other person, are wrong or have handled things badly.

If we are really honest with ourselves, we know that we make these mistakes quite often. We end up hurting people we love, blaming others for our misfortunes, letting down people who have trusted us and perhaps offering hollow apologies.

Learning to take better emotional responsibility means understanding why we keep repeating these errors, and taking steps to correct them. It does also, of course, mean accepting that we are fallible human beings, and that it is part of being human to sometimes get things wrong. This is also taking responsibility, but in a slightly different way. It is taking responsibility for the fact that we are not perfect, and that this is okay.

The games people play

Eric Berne, the founder of a therapeutic model called Transactional Analysis, very effectively explains why we make the emotional mistakes we do. In his book, *Games People Play*, Berne suggests that if you focus on the various conversational transactions that take place every day between people, you will notice some patterns. Some people become threatening to get what they want. Others turn someone's efforts at a serious conversation into a joke. Some people try very hard to make someone else feel guilty, or to present themselves as a victim. Berne notices that these conversations usually end up with someone feeling emotionally distressed – sad, angry, controlled, frightened, etc. Berne refers to these errors as 'the games people play'. In contrast, conversations that go smoothly make people feel good. These conversations are free of games.

When we play emotional games, we tend to take on one of the following three roles:

* **Rescuers** take care of people who should be taking care of themselves – taking responsibility for their

well-being, arguing on their behalf, letting them off the hook, preventing them from making their own decisions or from finding their own way.

* **Persecutors** tend to criticize, preach and punish. They want to verbally beat people into submission in order to get their own way or simply to prove they are superior.
* **Victims** are generally incapable of making any decisions at all, letting others run their lives and take care of them. This becomes a downward spiral of dependency and victimhood. The less a person does, the less they are capable of, and the more they require other people to run their lives for them.

This isn't to say that, on occasion, adopting one of these roles isn't emotionally sensible. However, when we use them to manipulate a relationship, such roles become harmful and unproductive.

Learning to take emotional responsibility

Taking emotional responsibility doesn't mean 'getting it right' all the time. We know enough now to understand that our emotional brain sometimes rides roughshod over reasonableness, and we often look back on a trail of emotional destruction. In the aftermath, our rational brain kicks back in, and we may thoroughly regret how we behaved. This is normal and natural – we are not suggesting that any of us become super-human beings who never put an emotional foot wrong.

Taking emotional responsibility asks only that we learn from our mistakes and attempt to fix emotional damage by making an effort to define and admit the faults and errors we have committed.

The art of apologizing

The thought of making a deeply felt apology strikes terror into the heart of the average person. They will consider an apology as 'losing face', backing off, allowing the other person to 'win', and they will consider it weak or humiliating. Yet the opposite is in fact true.

How to apologize

Even when understanding the principle, 'Sorry' can be the hardest word to say – especially when we don't really feel it. Taking emotional responsibility in a relationship doesn't mean taking the role of:

* victim – 'It was all my fault.'

Or:

* rescuer – 'It wasn't my fault, but I'll take the blame anyway to make you feel better.'

It means, very often, simply being the bigger person and being willing to be the one to own an error of judgement.

Here are four steps to help you:

1 **Be willing to admit to yourself that you have made a mistake.** This can be a difficult starting point because it can mean accepting your own inadequacies – 'What an idiot I am.' 'Now look what I've done.' etc. However, as you go through the full process of taking emotional responsibility, these feelings will be replaced by those of confidence and well-being.
2 **Be willing to admit your mistake to others.** Not only are we beating ourselves up for making an error, but we are exposing ourselves to the wrath or disappointment of others! Learn to overcome this fear. You will discover that admitting mistakes is an empowering experience and a key factor in becoming an emotionally intelligent being. Others recognize the courage it takes to apologize and will usually think much better of you for having done so.
3 **Convey genuine regret.** You will need to develop empathy before you can convey genuine regret. This is not just about saying sorry, it is about expressing a genuine understanding

of how the other person may be feeling due to what has happened. Only when another person feels that you really understand their view will your apology feel genuine to them, and be genuine to you.

4 **Put things right when you can.** Taking responsibility for a mistake usually means making amends of some sort. How to achieve this may not be obvious, and you don't need to have all the answers. The simple question 'How can I put this right?' or 'Is there any way that I can make amends?' is making amends in itself. You don't have to offer a solution. Asking someone to suggest what you can do is just as effective, possibly more so, and it suggests a willingness to put things right 'their way' rather than 'your way'. Making amends must, in any event, be something you and the person you are apologizing to decide between you, so that you achieve a mutually positive outcome.

Developing forgiveness

An inability to forgive will damage, or bring to an end, many personal and work-based relationships. How often do we hear someone say, 'I will never forgive her for that' or 'I will never get over what he did to me'? Nonetheless, forgiveness is not easy, especially when we feel that we have been grievously harmed, and we often hold on to the grudge and let it eat away at us over a period of years, if not a lifetime.

However, forgiveness is worthy of negotiation. Where we have been badly hurt emotionally, we do have the right to express to the person who has hurt us that our forgiveness may be dependent on their being willing to understand the pain they have caused. It is much easier for us to forgive harm that someone has done to us if they are willing to acknowledge the harm they have done. However, this is not always possible and then we are faced with a decision to make.

My fault or theirs?

Bear in mind that many grievances we harbour in personal relationships are subjective. In other words, we see a person's behaviour one way – they see it another.

The emotionally intelligent value of compassion

Compassion for others is essential to EI, but stirring up compassion in ourselves is not always easy.

Is compassion different from empathy? It essentially arises through empathy, and it could perhaps be called 'empathy in action'. It is using empathy – an understanding of someone's plight – in a practical way by offering some kind of physical or emotional support. In other words, compassion is an emotion that embraces a sense of shared suffering, most often combined with a desire to alleviate or reduce the suffering of someone else as if it were one's own.

Many years ago, compassion was described to me as 'the ability to feel your pain in my heart'. I have always felt this definition would be hard to better.

Exercise 18

The EI skill of other-awareness will assist you to develop compassion. Look around you. Be more aware of the lives of others. Every day, life gives us innumerable chances to open our hearts, if we can only take them. An old woman passes you with a sad and lonely face and two heavy bags full of shopping she can hardly carry. Stop for a moment and absorb what you see and become aware of your emotions. (You may even decide to help her with her shopping – active compassion.) Switch on the television, and see on the news a mother in a war-torn country kneeling beside the body of her murdered son, or an old grandmother in a developing country trying to sip the thin soup that is her only food.

In the moment you feel compassion within you, don't brush it aside or shrug it off and try quickly to return to 'normal'. Don't be afraid of your feeling or be embarrassed by it, and don't allow yourself to be distracted from it. Use that quick, bright rush of compassion – focus on it, develop it, enhance and deepen it.

Is there anything you feel that you might like to do to actively change the life of someone else for the better – even in the smallest way? This is the beginning of empathy in action.

It is hard to expose yourself to the plights of others, but actively doing so, and then identifying your emotions, will develop your compassionate nature and enable you to connect more closely with those close to you, who form part of your own life.

Learning to become non-judgemental

Increasing emotional intelligence by decreasing judgement

Being judgemental is such a subtle characteristic that most of us do not realize that we have it. It seems completely natural to us to develop views on anything and everything – which is perfectly healthy, of course – and we do not realize that we can slip into what is called 'negative bias' when relating to others.

There are two problems associated with harbouring judgemental views of others:

1. We become narrow thinkers ourselves. We decide that because we think something, that makes it a fact. We can also become naturally critical – instead of noticing someone's nice hairstyle, we focus on their inappropriate footwear. This negative bias prevents us from relating to people positively and cheerfully.
2. We fail to connect with others in a warm and empathetic way. If others feel that we may be critical of them, they will probably avoid us or adopt a defensive stance when talking to us.

Judgemental people try to foist their beliefs, their habits and their way of life on others. They are critical of people who don't see life the way they do. 'But my way feels right,' you may say. Well, your way feels right to you because of who you are, and it *is* right for you. Yet it is arrogant to think that others should always see things in the same way that you do. For all of our differences, as long as we aren't causing harm and havoc, we deserve love, respect and acceptance. The antidote to being judgemental is to become open-minded.

Learning to achieve open-mindedness

In the same way that a person who misuses alcohol may need to stop drinking totally, your own way forward is to stop judging – totally. You must stop evaluating others as being good or bad, right or wrong.

This will require a great deal of willpower and commitment, but the rewards will be enormous. As you stop judging others, you stop judging yourself. You will see that we cannot quantify good or bad, right or wrong. Our views are almost always subjective, and learning acceptance of them will be quite empowering.

7

emotional intelligence and others: developing good communication skills

It is easy to take communicating for granted. We can all do that, can't we? Well, yes and no. Emotionally intelligent communicating involves more than just passing information across. It involves doing this in a way that is positive and enabling for the person you are communicating with. It means dialogue – listening and understanding in a way that the other person knows and can appreciate. In negotiation, it doesn't simply mean bringing someone round to your point of view but in finding common ground where you are both comfortable. It means becoming someone people find easy to talk to as well as someone who can share how they feel in an open and non-judgemental way. In difficult situations, it means being able to use emotionally intelligent communication to make a good outcome more likely.

While some of you may believe you already possess good communication skills, this chapter will help you to hone these and to ensure that others share your view!

The importance of emotionally intelligent communication

Communication is the most important skill in life. We spend most of our waking hours communicating. If you wish to attend, there are myriad courses you can sign up for on effective communication skills that cover public speaking, presentation giving – anything where you have to stand up and speak to get your message across. This is important of course – you need people to understand you and your message. But what about listening? What about understanding what others have to say? Try to find a course on listening rather than speaking and you will be hard pressed. Listening is not highly regarded as a skill we should develop. Yet it is the most essential part of effective communication, of developing deep and meaningful personal and work-based relationships, of simply understanding people and their viewpoints.

Communicating well and listening actively is a key component of emotional intelligence. 'Other-awareness' isn't simply observing and appreciating, it requires a strong ability to both express yourself clearly and to attend to and understand others fully.

Think about the reasons we need to communicate:

* to pass on information
* to ask for what we want
* to share how we feel
* to understand how others feel
* to achieve goals and outcomes.

If we learn to communicate well, we are more likely to achieve successful outcomes in any given situation, which equals being emotionally intelligent.

How to learn the art of skilled listening

In his book *How to Turn People into Gold*, American author Kenneth Goode says 'Stop a minute to contrast your keen interest in your own affairs with your mild concern about anything else.

Realize then, that everybody else in the world feels exactly the same way! Then, along with Lincoln and Roosevelt, you will have grasped the only solid foundation for inter-personal relationships: namely, that success in dealing with people depends on a sympathetic grasp of the other person's viewpoint.'

Be actively present

Most people, when they listen, are not actively present with the other person. Most people are either talking, or they are simply waiting for the other person to finish speaking so that they can speak again. When we don't listen effectively we:

* annoy those who are giving us their time
* fail to hear vital information being given
* fail to grasp the other person's point of view
* lose ground in negotiating well
* weaken relationships.

Exercise 19

Some common listening weaknesses include the following. Place a cross next to any you consider apply to you:

- ☐ Getting distracted by thoughts that are nothing to do with what the other person is talking about.
- ☐ Interrupting and breaking the other person's train of thought.
- ☐ Making meaningless comments, such as 'Oh, I'm sure it will all work out right in the end.'
- ☐ Minimizing what is being said – 'Oh, I wouldn't get too upset about that if I were you.'
- ☐ Starting to show restlessness if the other person takes a while to tell their story.
- ☐ Agreeing too quickly with statements, simply to get the conversation moved on.
- ☐ Cutting in and giving advice, rather than letting the other person work through their thought processes.
- ☐ Stopping listening and spending your time planning what you will say as soon as you get a chance to speak.

☐ Actively attempting to drive the conversation in a particular direction – perhaps directing it to your own problems rather than the speaker's.

If you have more than one or two crosses, then you need to work much harder on your listening skills.

Pay total attention

Show your interest by stopping all other activities. If the conversation is important, do everything you can to ensure that you will not be interrupted unnecessarily – close the door, suspend phone calls, tell others that you do not wish to be interrupted – and turn off your mobile phone.

Keep eye contact

It is vital that, when someone is speaking to you, you look directly at them. It conveys interest and respect – whereas constantly looking away conveys the opposite. This does not mean staring intently at someone, which can of course be exceedingly uncomfortable for both of you. It means maintaining appropriate eye contact, and looking away only briefly, from time to time.

Show positive responses

Responses can be both verbal and non-verbal (nods, hand movements, facially expressing interest) but however you do it, you must show that you received the message – and more importantly, show that it had an impact on you.

Even out the cadence of your voice

Speak at roughly the same energy level as the other person – then they'll know they really got through and don't have to keep repeating themselves.

Show understanding

To say 'I understand' is not enough. People need some sort of evidence that you have truly understood. Prove your understanding by occasionally summarizing the basis of their idea ('It sounds as though you really do want to go for that promotion') or by asking a question that proves you have grasped the main idea ('So if you decide to do this, what sort of timescale are you thinking of?'). The important point is not to repeat what they've said to prove you were listening, but to show you understand the point and purpose of what they are telling you.

Respect others' views

Show that you take the views of others seriously. It seldom helps to tell people 'I appreciate your position' or 'I know how you feel', although don't dismiss these comments out of hand – they can be useful if you really are uncertain what to say, and if silence would be awkward. However, you really want to show respect by communicating with others at their level of understanding and attitude. You can do this by adjusting your tone of voice, rate of speech and choice of words to show that you are trying to empathize with the speaker's position.

Listening to and acknowledging other people may seem deceptively simple, but doing it well, particularly when disagreements arise, takes true talent. As with any skill, listening well takes plenty of practice.

Make sure not just that you understand, but that others feel understood

We usually feel most heard when someone reflects back to us what we have just said. For example, 'It sounds as though you are really struggling at present. Tom's away a great deal and with three children under five, it is often too much to cope with on your own.' The relief of being able to say, 'Yes, that's exactly how it is.' And knowing that you have been listened to and understood creates great respect and closeness between two people.

This is not an easy skill to master, and it does not come naturally to most people without a great deal of practice.

Exercise 20

Here are two examples of conversations where you have alternative responses. Decide for yourself which response reflects the speaker's viewpoint, and which the listener's.

1 **Speaker:** My boss has laid off my assistant at work, and I really don't know how I am going to manage without her.
Response A: *Oh dear. That's just what you need right now, on top of all the other problems you have.*
Response B: *I'm sorry about that. It sounds as though you are going to find things more difficult now that you have no one to help you.*

2 **Speaker:** I'm concerned about my relationship. Bill is behaving very distantly just now, and I'm not sure what's wrong.
Response A: *Tell me about it! Jim does this to me all the time. I don't think there's anything wrong. It's just the way men are sometimes.*
Response B: *I'm sorry to hear about that. It must be difficult not knowing why Bill is being distant right now.*

What we are looking at here is the difference between responses that are:

a focused on the speaker, or
b self-centred.

A criticism of reflected responding is that it simply repeats what the speaker has been saying. However, there is a very good reason for doing this – it lets the other person continue with their own train of thought. You may yourself have experienced situations where you start to tell someone something that is important to you, but never get to finish what you wish to say as the listener has either asked a question that has taken the conversation off in another direction, or they have told you about a similar experience of their own. None of this is the end of the world – and of course we all do it from time to time. But where a person has something serious to say, reflective listening is an important and emotionally intelligent way of ensuring that that person has the opportunity and the space to speak and be heard.

Learn the value of summarizing

Summarizing is an important skill to ensure that you and the person you are talking to are still having the same conversation! Never merely assume that you have got the gist of what is being said – summarize what you believe you have heard. It is also important as, on occasions, we all tell our stories in over-long and rambling ways, with various side turnings and cul-de-sacs that may, or may not, be important to the central theme. Your summary is therefore like a précis of what has gone before.

How you can do this

You can start a summary, which should only be one or two sentences long, with phrases such as:

* Let me just be sure I have understood that. You're ...
* OK. It sounds as though what's happened is ...
* Tell me if I'm wrong, but I think you're saying that ...
* If I've understood correctly, there's ...

Summarizing has three great pluses:

* Like reflecting, it ensures that the speaker feels heard.
* It ensures that you haven't got the wrong end of the stick.
* It gives the speaker an opportunity to correct you if you have, or add further information to give clarity.

Body language – understanding the non-verbal messages you give out

'It's not what you say, it's the way that you say it' is a famous line, and we all understand what it means. Non-verbal messages are an essential component of communication. Most people assume that what we have to say is communicated mainly via what comes out of our mouths. Have a guess at the following:

Write down, in percentage terms, how much of our communication is via

* The words we say _____
* Our tone of voice _____
* Our body language _____

What have you put?

Here is the answer:

The words we utter account for roughly 10 per cent of our communication. Our tone of voice accounts for 25 per cent, and our body language a staggering 65 per cent. Before you dismiss this, consider a couple of examples.

> You walk into a restaurant with a friend. As you sit down, you see a couple across the room. You cannot hear a word they are saying, but you notice some gesticulations and an angry look on the face of one of the diners, whilst the other one looks away and makes no eye contact. What would you assume is going on? Very likely, some sort of argument. But you didn't hear a word.
>
> Picture the same scenario, but this time, the couple are leaning towards each other, their eye contact is obvious, and they are smiling. Now make another assumption. This time, I suspect you will guess that they are deeply connected, and possibly in a loving relationship. You still haven't heard a word.
>
> **Now flashback to your childhood.** Earlier in the day you were working on a project in the dining room that involved scissors and glue, and you have a rather nasty feeling that some of the glue may have found its way on to the surface of the highly polished dining table. You have decided to say nothing and hope that it won't be noticed. Now you are upstairs in your room, and your mother is downstairs. You hear your name called. Just your name. Nothing else. You will almost certainly be able to tell immediately from the tone of your mother's voice whether (a) she is alerting you to the fact that your favourite TV programme is on, or (b) she has found the glue adhered to the dining table. Again, no words have been uttered, other than your name. In this case, tone of voice was the giveaway.

Most of us are more expert in reading body language than we realize, as the above examples may have shown. We can usually pick up whether someone is happy or sad, tense or relaxed. However, there are, of course, two aspects to our Non-Verbal Communications (NVC):

* our ability to read the messages that others are giving us
* the messages we give out.

Many of us are less expert at assessing the messages that we give others, yet this is an enormously important part of social interaction. Here is a common conversation:

Mary: I've been telling you about my day and you are obviously not at all interested.

Jane: No, really, I'm hugely interested.

Mary: Well, you don't look interested at all!

Jane's NVC had obviously given her away! Think about the different characteristics of NVC that might enable you to become a more accurate giver and receiver of non-verbal messages. For example:

* eye contact
* facial expressions
* gestures
* posture and body orientation
* proximity
* humour.

Using your eyes

We have already spoken about the importance of good eye contact. Don't overlook this. When you make eye contact you open the flow of communication and convey interest, concern, warmth and credibility.

Smiling

Smile! Smiling is a powerful cue that transmits:

* happiness
* friendliness
* warmth
* liking
* affiliation.

If you smile frequently you will be perceived as more likable, friendly, warm and approachable. Smiling is often contagious and others will react positively to you.

Gestures

Some of us can gesture quite a lot when we are speaking. We wave our hands and use specific facial expressions, nod our heads, etc. It makes what we say come alive. If you fail to gesture while speaking, you may be perceived as boring, stiff and unanimated. Gestures will make you appear more animated, as well as indicate that you are listening.

Standing tall

The way you walk, talk, stand and sit tells other people a great deal. Standing in a relaxed way and leaning slightly forward communicates that you are approachable, receptive and friendly. A feeling of closeness results when you and another person face each other. Speaking with your back turned or looking at the floor or ceiling is – very obviously! – going to communicate disinterest.

Don't get too close

We need to have an awareness of invading someone's space – simply getting too close to them physically. Sometimes we lean towards people who are speaking softly, but that can be perceived as over-closeness. It is better to be open, and invite them to 'speak up'.

Mirroring

Matching your body language to the speaker will help to give you further rapport. If they lean forward, do the same. If they lower the tone of their voice, adjust yours as well. This is especially useful if you are having a difficult conversation with someone. Using matching, or mirroring, works extremely well in keeping things calm and you are more likely to reach a satisfactory conclusion to the topic under discussion. Try it and see.

Insight

Never underestimate the power of NVC when relating to others. You can communicate intimately and positively with someone on an emotional level without saying a word.

Becoming more assertive

Sometimes, the conversations we have are not easy. They are not about us happily listening to someone else recounting the details of their Italian holiday – or even seeking our advice with their problems. In those dialogues we are either in neutral mode or in control of the conversation.

What about difficult conversations, where we need every skill we possess not to allow things to descend into a disagreement? What you say, and how you say it, will decide whether you achieve a good (emotionally intelligent) outcome or feel stressed and upset when the conversation ends.

What is your personal style? Do you tend to be:

* passive ('Oh, all right then.')
* aggressive ('Because I say so, that's why.')
* assertive ('I'd like to help, but I'm too busy right now.')?

Unless you are already naturally assertive, developing this communication style will help you to defuse difficult conversations and remain emotionally in touch with the person you are having difficulties with.

The features of an assertive style

An assertive communication style means that you are:

* keen to find a solution to problems where everyone is happy
* strong enough to stand up calmly for your own rights
* able to accept without rancour that others have rights too
* interested in the other person's point of view.

Two major reasons for choosing to negotiate assertively are:

1 It is usually *effective*. Quite simply, you are more likely to get the outcome you want.
2 It is the style that *others appreciate the most*. Therefore, they are less likely to avoid negotiating with you because they can rely on you remaining calm and looking for a good outcome for both of you.

Your emotional rights

A major feature of assertiveness is that you do have the right to say how you feel. The passive person fails to say how they feel, and the aggressor will not own their feelings, but will suggest that you *'made'* them feel that way. Being assertive means saying 'I feel very unhappy when you speak to me like that' as opposed to 'You make me very unhappy when you speak to me like that.' This may seem like a finely tuned play on words, but it is actually emphasizing an important difference. You are taking responsibility for how you feel but, at the same time, explaining that their actions are creating these feelings in you.

Stand your ground

Staying calm and standing firm at the same time takes a lot of practice, but is well worth the effort. In order to do this, you need to keep things simple, and operate on a three-step basis.

Here is a sample situation:

Jenny's teenage daughter Donna wants to go to a pop concert and stay overnight with her boyfriend. Jenny isn't at all happy about this request. However, rather than simply saying 'no' (and at the very least causing resentment, or at worst, a big row), Jenny does the following:

1 She acknowledges Donna's request and feeling:
'I appreciate how important and exciting this would be for you, and how much you must be looking forward to it.'
2 Then Jenny states her own reservations.
'However, I am concerned for you staying overnight as you are only 14, so I am going to say 'no' to that.'

3 Finally, Jenny offers a solution.
'Still, I know you really want to go to the concert, so why don't we arrange for a cab to bring you home which will give you the time to have a drink and a chat afterwards, before leaving?'

Notice the three steps:

1 Acknowledge.
2 Use 'but' or 'however' to state how you feel.
3 Offer an alternative solution where you can.

The 'broken record' technique

Of course, the situation above is in an ideal world of instant compliance. In the real world, Donna would be saying, 'Oh, but Mum ...' and continuing to argue her case. In that case, you use the 'broken record' technique, which is exactly as it sounds. No matter how Donna pleads, Jenny keeps repeating her terms. She consistently acknowledges what Donna is saying: 'I am sorry that you are so disappointed with my decision.' 'I appreciate how cross you are that I am not going along with this.' Then Jenny will repeat her 'But' or 'However' and restate steps 2 and 3.

If you use this skill well, sooner or later, the other person will accept your terms and you will both feel happy with the outcome (the average 'come back' before the other person concedes is two to three times, so you can afford to wait it out).

Keeping an eye on the outcome

Achieving a 'win:win' result

Stephen Covey, in his book *The Seven Habits of Highly Effective People*, coins a phrase that has since become popular when negotiating. He calls it a 'Win:Win situation'. He identifies four possible outcomes to negotiations:

1 You win/they lose.
2 They win/you lose.
3 You both lose (no deal).
4 You both win.

Until Covey flagged up the pluses of win:win, most people thought of 'winning' in a verbal negotiation as meaning that the other person lost. An emotionally intelligent, elegant solution to a controversy, however, needs an outcome that everyone feels is fair. This requires many EI qualities and skills being used in abundance in order to keep a negotiation on the table until all the options have been explored and the most suitable one agreed on. This might well (and often does) mean compromise. Nonetheless, where this is equal, or where one person gives one thing in order to gain another, compromise is very definitely win:win.

Yet sometimes the ideal of win:win does not happen, and Covey adds a corollary to this with 'Win:Win/No Deal' as the full negotiating tool. In other words, win/lose or lose/win are not emotionally intelligent options. Either you negotiate to the happy agreement of both parties, or you put it all aside for another day.

Conclusion

Emotional intelligence – not just the what, but the how

There is an abundance of definitions of emotional intelligence, and some are quoted here. Perhaps the easiest to appreciate is Daniel Goleman's idea that it is 'Just plain getting along with people.' To most of us, this is an important ideal that we constantly strive for, with all its rewards.

What this book has attempted to show you is how you acquire EI yourself. I would also like to place this 'how' in layperson's terms. EI requires you simply to step into another person's shoes, to see the world through their eyes. To do this, you will need to ask yourself questions such as:

* 'How would I feel/think about that if I were them?'
* 'What would I be saying if I were advising this person?'
* 'What are this person's wishes and hopes?'

You will start developing what I call 'other-awareness' quickly and easily. This is the basis for emotionally intelligent thinking.

Self-awareness requires open-mindedness. It means not only understanding and identifying how we are thinking and feeling, but being willing to expand our repertoire, as it were, asking questions such as:

* 'Are there any other ways I can look at this?'
* 'Does that thought really matter?'
* 'What might be the outcome(s) for me of thinking this way?'

Developing retrospective learning

One of the frustrations of attempting to make personal development changes is that, in the heat of the moment, we forget or are unable to recall quickly enough the new EI skills we are trying to acquire. Don't worry. This is fine. To move forward, simply apply retrospective learning until your brain can assimilate these new skills as its default. Retrospective learning means looking back at what happened and asking yourself 'What can I learn from this?' For example, if you felt that things went wrong – that you handled something badly, or the result wasn't what you'd hoped for – you can ask yourself 'What could I have done differently to get a better outcome?' Equally, while we often omit to do this, when something has gone well, it is good to look back at that too, and work out what you did that contributed to the positive outcome so that you can carry it with you into the future. To take this learning seriously, write your answers down on paper. This helps your brain absorb these new ideas more firmly. Spend time on this.

Exercise 21

To help your EI learning, replay a difficult situation in your mind. Imagine that what happened was recorded on a video recorder. Imagine yourself replaying the video – literally watching it on TV – but in slow motion this time, and notice the points at which you might have behaved differently. Take your time. Write down what you notice and see, and use vision to come up with a new way of dealing with such an event, should it recur.

Visualization

You can also plan ahead of time. Where there is something coming up that is important to you, where you want to achieve the best outcome and where you need to use your EI skills to their best, take the time to sit quietly and simply imagine this happening. You can start your visualization well before the event:

* Picture what you might decide to wear.
* Picture what you will be doing beforehand.
* Notice your environment – become really absorbed in where you are, and be able to picture it clearly.
* Move on to the moment you are thinking of where you wish to achieve your best outcome. If it is a conversation,

picture what the other person will be looking like, how their demeanour might be, where you will be meeting – again, absorb the atmosphere in detail.

* If you are in a room together, notice pictures on the wall, the location of the furniture. Really *be* there.
* Now think of what you will do and say, and also what the other person is likely to do or say.
* Replay the visualization with a variety of different scenarios, and picture how you will deal with each of them.
* Ideally, depending on the importance of the occasion, do this several times so that you feel that you have practised well and will be confident when the reality comes along.

You can use visualization for more general life goals too. Start to think about what you want from your life and your future and use visualization to imagine yourself both getting there and being there.

Visualization is a wonderful skill – used by many top business people and sports people when they picture themselves succeeding, which then makes the actuality both easier (virtual practice) and more likely (self-belief).

How to activate change

The people who get the most out of life choose to make the decision to take action that will result in change. Sometimes, external events, and the outcomes of those events, provide a catalyst that causes people to get started. For others, they cannot wait to become proactive, and it is more a case of understanding the right direction to go in. They simply decide that life can be better and feel determined to make that change. This is what you now need to do yourself.

I hope that you now know enough about the positive benefits of EI to make similar choices. You have worked through this book so you are at least part of the way there. If you have not yet worked through the activities and exercises, note down those that you feel will be important to you, and that will make a difference.

If you can manage yourself effectively, then you will have no trouble becoming emotionally intelligent. You will understand yourself. You will have passion and a sense of purpose, and you will relate well to others, providing understanding, empathy and enthusiasm that will enable connection and intimacy.

Exercise 22

To help you assess your own competencies and those you would like to have, here is a summary of the well-researched key components of EI. Appreciate that every commentator has their own version of what they consider to be most important, and there is some flexibility here. Don't worry if you see slightly different lists in different books: it is often just a different way of saying the same, or a similar, thing.

Your goal is to assess those competencies that you consider you may already have, and highlight those that you may not have but would like to have, based on what you now understand of their importance, and the work that would be involved in achieving such skills.

Self-awareness
Emotional self-awareness
Accurate self-assessment
Self-confidence

Self-management
Self-control
Trustworthiness
Conscientiousness
Adaptability
Desire to achieve
Initiative
Building bonds

Social awareness
Empathy
Organizational awareness
Willingness to help others

Social skills
Developing others
Leadership
Influence
Communication
Ability to generate change
Conflict management
Teamwork

Adapted from Richard Boyatziz, 1999

In a nutshell, you are looking to achieve an ability to define your goals, be positively motivated to achieve them, maintain positive relationships with others and have good awareness of your personal strengths and weaknesses and how to harness these.

You have emotional intelligence within you. It is there, at the ready. You simply need to become competent in activating it. You will. Good luck.